IDENTITY
&GENDER

OUR
VALUES

by
Charlie Ogden

THE SECRET BOOK COMPANY

©2020
The Secret Book Company
King's Lynn, Norfolk PE30 4LS

ISBN: 978-1-78998-072-1

Written by:
Charlie Ogden

Edited by:
Grace Jones

Designed by:
Drue Rintoul

A catalogue record for this book is available from the British Library.

All facts, statistics, web addresses and URLs in this book were verified as valid and accurate at time of writing. No responsibility for any changes to external websites or references can be accepted by either the author or publisher.

Photo Credits
Abbreviations: l–left, r–right, b–bottom, t–top, c–centre, m–middle.

Front Cover & 1 – lazyllama, Rawpixel.com, ESB Professional, InesBazdar. 2 – Rawpixel.com. 4 – Ollyy. 5 – Eugenio M 6 – paul prescott. 7 – conrado. 8 – William Perugini. 9t – Vadim Georgiev. 9b – Alex Brylov. 10 – Yuriy Rudyy. 11 – 50 12 – Monkey Business Images. 13 – Ollyy. 14 – Dmytro Zinkevych. 15 – Brian A Jackson. 16 – lynea. 17l – Andresr. 17 g-stockstudio. 18 – Rawpixel.com. 19 – anekoho. 20 – Viacheslav Nikolaenko. 21 – oceanfishing. 22 – Everett Histor – VSForever. 23m – PHOTOCREO Michal Bednarek. 24 – Everett Collection. 25 – Everett Historical. 26 – szefei. 27 – 28 – J. Bicking. 29 – everst. 30t – Rawpixel.com. 30ml – Antonio Gravante. 30mr – Dmytro Zinkevych. 30b – Ditty summer. Images are courtesy of Shutterstock.com, unless stated otherwise. With thanks to Getty Images, Thinks and iStockphoto.

CONTENTS

Words that look like **this** can be found in the glossary on page 31.

WHAT IS IDENTITY?

Every person on the planet has an identity. Identities are the views that people have of themselves; they are the ways that people think about and see themselves. What a person believes and feels strongly about in life can often make up a large part of their identity. This is because people often feel that what they believe in makes up a large part of who they are.

A person's identity is not always something that you can see. In fact, in a lot of cases, a person's identity is only known to them. Identities grow over time and can be shaped by a lot of different things – some that you can control and some that you can't control. There are a lot of different parts to a person's identity, but basically, your identity is the collection of things that make you, you!

Your identity is the view that you have of yourself and it develops over time.

ANIMAL RIGHTS

An example of something that could be part of your identity is caring about animal rights. People who care about animal rights believe that there should be laws to stop people from mistreating animals. In many places around the world, animals live in terrible conditions – they are kept in very small cages and are sometimes not given enough food or water.

Animal rights **activists** often go to **protests** or write **articles** in order to try to prevent animals around the world from being mistreated. These people have very strong beliefs about animal rights and spend a lot of their time trying to help animals, so these people can often feel that animal rights are a part of their identity.

Animal rights activists often hold protests to raise awareness about the mistreatment of animals.

GROUP IDENTITIES

Sometimes a large group of people can share an identity. When a lot of people gather together to celebrate a belief or a **tradition**, they could be said to have a group identity.

These people share a group identity as they all follow the Hindu religion.

One of the most common ways that people can share a group identity is through religion. People who follow the same religion could be said to have a group identity. This is because they share **fundamental** beliefs about the world and the way they should live their lives. However, to have a shared identity does not mean that you have the exact same identity as someone else. Everyone's identity is special and **unique** to them. This means that a person can have their own personal identity and share a group identity at the same time.

IDENTITY THROUGH TIME

A person's identity often takes a long time to develop and be fully understood. This is because a person needs to know a lot about themselves before they can really understand their identity and who they are as a person. People often need to have a lot of experiences before they realise what is important to them and what they believe in. Because of this, it can take a long time for a person to understand their identity. **Physical attributes** and hobbies can influence your identity, too. For example, when people get older, their hobbies and interests might change. However, your hobbies and physical attributes aren't the only part of your identity – there are many other things that make up who we are.

Our identities can change throughout our lifetimes.

WHAT SHAPES YOUR IDENTITY?

A person's identity can be shaped by a huge range of different things. Experiences, people, places, conversations and music can all influence someone's identity. Identities are shaped by things you can control and things you can't control, such as your **genetics**.

People's identities have been shaped by music for many years.

Knowing what has shaped your identity can be very difficult. However, it is important that people think about what has shaped them as a person as this can help people to understand their identity.

This is because if you know what things in your past have made you into the person you are today, you will know what things in life are most important to you.

PASSIONS

A person's passions are the things that they are most enthusiastic about. Everybody has passions – such as games, music, books, countries and animals – and often a person's passions make up a large part of their identity. For example, people who are very passionate about saving the environment will often make this passion a part of their identity.

The things that we are interested in and passionate about can often change as we grow older. This is how your identity can develop and grow over time. As your passions change, certain parts of your identity change as well. However, while certain aspects of your identity will change, grow and develop, many people believe that there is a core part of your identity that will always stay the same. It is this core part of your identity that means that you will always be you, no matter what passions you follow later on in life.

FAMILIES

Members of your family, and the people who raised you, will often have a big influence on your identity. This isn't surprising, as the people who raise us teach us a lot about life and how the world works.

One way that parents and guardians can shape the identities of their children is by helping them to understand what is right and wrong. This helps children to develop a sense of **morality**. Parents and guardians regularly tell their children when they have done something bad and explain to them why it was wrong. People often remember these lessons about what is right and wrong and use them throughout their lives to work out what is right.

Parents and guardians often pass on their passions to their children – so if cycling is a part of your father's identity, it might become a part of yours, too!

CULTURES

Cultures are the ideas, **customs** and behaviours that a particular group of people are used to. Cultures can often involve such things as the food that people eat, the languages that people speak and the way that people act. A person's culture might come from the country or area where they live, and the people they are around.

Paper lanterns are an important part of Japanese culture.

People might inherit their cultural identity from their parents. A person doesn't have to live in a particular country to feel that it is part of their cultural identity. You can experience the culture of a place through the traditions, people, food and celebrations.

Sharing the same culture is another way in which people can have a group identity. People from the same culture often follow the same religion, celebrate the same festivals and take part in the same traditions.

A person's culture usually involves many things that they see as important, which is why culture often becomes a part of a person's identity. When people have a group identity through culture, they are said to have a cultural identity.

BEING HAPPY WITH WHO YOU ARE

There are lots of things in life that make people happy, such as tasty food, nice clothes and going on holiday. However, most people believe that being happy with who you are takes more than just going on holiday. Being happy with who you are involves being happy with the way that you act and the things that you do.

The first step to being happy with who you are is thinking about what is important to you. Once you have worked this out, you can start to live a life that you are happy with. For example, Max knows that the most important thing in her life is football – she can't think of anything she wants more than to be a professional football player. Because of this, a good way for Max to be happy with her life and who she is would be to practise football every day.

Playing football is a good way for Max to be happy with who she is because it helps Max to achieve her dream of becoming a professional football player. Thinking about your hobbies, passions and what you enjoy can help you to be happy with who you are. As you get older, these hobbies and passions might become part of your future identity.

But don't worry, you don't have to think about your future identity or what you want to be when you grow up to be happy with who you are now. If you like playing the piano, keep practising! If you prefer maths, keep doing that instead!

A big part of being happy with who you are is thinking about the things that make you happy and doing those things.

VALUES

Living your life according to the values that you believe in is one of the best ways to be happy with who you are. Values are things that people hold very strong views about, just like passions. However, values aren't things that you can see in the world, such as books, games and animals. Instead, a person's values are the types of behaviour that they think are most important, such as telling the truth, being kind and showing people **respect**.

Many people believe that being kind and generous is a very important value to live by.

A good way to be happy with who you are is to work out the values that are most important to you and to try to put them into practice in your day-to-day life. For example, you might think that it is very important for people to be kind and honest. Because of this, a good way for you to be happy with who you are would be for you to try to be as kind and honest as possible.

ACCEPTING WHO YOU ARE

There are some things about yourself that you can't change – and these might be things you wish you could change. There are lots of reasons you might not like things about yourself – someone might have said something mean about the way you look, or you might have been bullied for being different in some way. This doesn't mean you should change, though. Everyone is different, and these are the things that make us unique and special. Accepting that these things are part of your unique identity – and even learning to love them – will help you feel happy and proud of your identity. If anyone says something mean, you can ignore them – it would be boring if everyone was the same!

Learning to love yourself – and every single little thing that makes you a brilliant, unique YOU – will give you self-confidence and happiness. Accepting and embracing our gifts and struggles can he hard; but it's totally worth it. You're awesome, whatever your identity!

WHAT IS GENDER?

Gender is often seen as the difference between males and females. This is correct in some situations, however, to fully understand what gender means, we have to **contrast** it with 'sex'. 'Sex' is the **biological** difference between the body of a male and the body a female.

'Gender' is a **social construct**. This means that we have given male and female genders certain characteristics. These characteristics can be different depending on a society, culture or a period in time. These characteristics are not always right and can easily become **stereotypes**.

For example, in Victorian times, women were expected to behave in a certain way. They were stereotyped to be very kind and domestic. This was also known as being 'Angel in the House'.

Gender roles are when a particular gender is expected to take on a specific role within society. For example, this could be that a man must earn the money in the family and that a female must stay home and take care of the children. These roles are also stereotypes and do not have to be followed. Nowadays, more and more people are becoming much more accepting of others and less concerned with gender stereotypes and roles.

The social construct of gender expects men and women to behave differently and like different things. Things that men stereotypically like and do are called 'masculine' and things that women stereotypically like and do are called 'feminine'. However, any person can like and do more masculine or feminine things or be a mix of both. For example, some females might prefer wearing trousers instead of skirts and dresses even though this is stereotypically male clothing. Males might like to wear dresses and skirts even though this is stereotypically female. Some people might wear a mixture of both trousers and skirts.

Woman

Man

Unlike sex, a person's gender has nothing to do with their physical attributes. Instead, gender is determined by each person's individual relationship with the societies and cultures that are important to them. Because of this, there is no reason to think that boys should be masculine or girls should be feminine – be who you want to be!

IDENTITY AND GENDER

Identity and gender are very closely linked and a person's gender often makes up a large part of their identity.

It doesn't matter if you are part of a group identity or not - just be happy with who you are!

Identity isn't usually something that is shown on the outside – for example, you can't usually tell if someone is very passionate about animal rights just by looking at them. This can be the same with gender. You can't tell what a person's gender is just by looking at them. Just because a person looks like a boy, doesn't mean that they have a masculine gender.

It is important not to stereotype someone's gender based on how they look on the outside. Some people don't have one particular gender; these people might call themselves non-binary. Some people don't label themselves with a gender at all. Other people don't feel that their biological sex matches their gender identity. This is called being transgender.

GENDER IDENTITY

Every person on the planet has a gender identity. A person's gender identity is the way that they feel about their own gender and – just like a general identity – it often involves a lot of their beliefs, values, passions, likes and dislikes. A gender identity is a person's own experience of their gender and the way that they interact with the world.

The Thai flag

Thailand has one of the most accepting societies in the world in relation to gender identities. Views about masculinity and femininity aren't very strict in the country and people are mostly free to express their gender identity however they please.

Because some societies have very clear ideas about what gender should look like, some people who live in those societies have a difficult time figuring out their gender identity. Lots of societies are slowly realising that gender and sex are different, and it's fine to express yourself any way you like. Wherever you are in the world, we should support people who are exploring their gender identity so they are safe, respected and **equal**.

THE GENDER SPECTRUM

For a long time, people thought that a person's gender could be only one of two things – it had to be either masculine or feminine. This is because people still thought that gender was linked to sex, and that there were only two sexes: male and female. Nowadays, however, many people accept that gender should be thought of as a **spectrum**.

The colour spectrum

To better understand what the gender spectrum means, look at the colour spectrum. At one end of the spectrum there is violet and at the other end there is red. To say that a person's gender is either masculine or feminine is like saying that the only colours are violet and red. As we can see from this colour spectrum, there are many colours between violet and red. In the same way, there are a lot of different possible genders between masculinity and femininity.

The gender spectrum allows for many different expressions of gender. A person's identity might fall anywhere on the spectrum – someone might identify with one or several gender identities. Think about all the people you know. Do they have characteristics from just one of the genders? Of course not! Everyone is made up of lots of different characteristics that can be from different genders.

There is room on the gender spectrum for everyone, no matter what their gender identity and biological sex are. Whether a person has the gender that matches their sex, is the opposite to their sex or is a mixture of different genders, gender identity is different for everyone. We should understand that everyone needs to be true to themselves to be happy.

This is the genderqueer pride flag. It represents people who have gender identities that are non-binary.

HISTORY OF GENDER IDENTITY

In the past, people assumed that a person's gender was determined by their sex, meaning that all men had to be masculine and all women had to be feminine. Because of this, men and women throughout history have been **discriminated** against for their gender.

Throughout history, many people have challenged gender roles. One notable person to do this was Amelia Earhart, who, in 1932, was the first woman to fly across the Atlantic Ocean. At the time, most people expected only men to be pilots.

In the past, more people believed in specific gender roles for each sex. For example, in some places, men were expected to be fighters and workers, whereas women were expected to be mothers and carers. However, throughout history, people have been challenging the gender roles given to each sex. This is because, throughout time and in certain places, people did not understand that men and women could have **traits** that were outside of their gender roles.

The way that gender was understood changed in many ways throughout history. In ancient times, in places such as ancient Rome and ancient Greece, different genders were believed to possess different kinds of knowledge. This is similar to the way that gender roles were thought about, as the people in ancient Rome and ancient Greece believed that men had knowledge about fighting and crafting, whereas women had knowledge about emotions, care and healing.

HOWEVER, EVEN SOME GODS AND GODDESSES DIDN'T FIT THEIR GENDER ROLES. FOR EXAMPLE, THE ANCIENT GREEK GODDESS, ARTEMIS, WAS THE GODDESS OF THE HUNT AND WILD ANIMALS. THIS SUGGESTS THAT SHE HAD MASCULINE KNOWLEDGE AS WELL AS FEMININE.

Throughout history, people have stepped out of their gender roles and stereotypes. Unfortunately, breaking these roles and stereotypes is not always accepted or welcomed by a society. Luckily, this is beginning to change and a person's gender identity is becoming less focused on a person's biological sex.

Even in recent history, people have been commonly discriminated against because of their gender identity. Many **civilisations** that became powerful throughout history thought that men were better than women, which led to a lot of people being discriminated against for their sex and gender. In these societies, women were often treated badly because of their biological sex, regardless of their gender identity. As well as this, men were often only respected if they had a masculine gender identity. Many men and women were discriminated against because they had gender identities that didn't fit with the gender roles given to their biological sex.

Gender-based discrimination often occurred during wars. Women were often not allowed to be soldiers in wars as fighting was seen as a man's duty. On top of this, many men who did not want to fight were discriminated against for not being masculine enough.

Unfortunately, it is difficult to know exactly how non-binary and transgender people were treated throughout history as there were very few records kept about people's gender. However, this isn't because non-binary and transgender people didn't exist. Instead, it is likely that people were often afraid to express their gender identity because they were scared that they might be discriminated against.

OSCAR WILDE, A FAMOUS VICTORIAN PLAYWRIGHT, POET AND AUTHOR, WAS ONE OF THE FIRST CELEBRITIES TO CHALLENGE SOCIAL VIEWS ABOUT GENDER IN BOTH HIS WORK AND IN HIS LIFE.

Many societies started to become safer and more accepting places in the 1900s. Because of this, the number of people who identified as non-binary and transgender grew very quickly. While people were still often discriminated against for their gender identity, being transgender and non-binary was slowly becoming more accepted. This led to many people being more open about their gender identity.

GENDER TODAY

Governments from all around the world have passed laws to try to give people of any gender equal rights, equal opportunities and an equal status in their societies. In the UK, it is now illegal for someone to be refused a job or an education based on their gender identity. On top of this, people of any gender are allowed to marry each other. In 2004, the UK government also passed the Gender Recognition Act, which made it possible for a person to officially change their legal gender if they wanted to.

In recent years, lots of people have joined the gender neutrality movement. This is the idea that laws and languages should avoid distinguishing between different genders. This is because it promotes the old belief that there are only two genders, rather than gender being a spectrum.

The Indian flag

Many other governments have also made laws that try to make non-binary and transgender people feel more welcome and at home in their own country. One of these countries is India, which, in 2014, made 'transgender' the country's third official gender.

The Indian government did this because they believed that a person's gender identity is a core part of their right to freedom. They believed that people should always feel free to express their gender, no matter where their gender falls on the gender spectrum.

It is important for everyone in today's society to respect and accept people, no matter what their gender identity is. Understanding your gender identity can take a very long time and sometimes people can become very frustrated by it. Often, transgender and non-binary people are worried that their families and friends might not accept their gender identity. It is important to always treat people equally, no matter what their gender identity is, so that they feel comfortable and welcome in their community.

If you feel confused or curious about your gender identity, it can help to talk about it with someone. When you're with someone that you know and trust, talk to them about your gender identity and how it makes you feel. It is important to understand that your gender identity is normal and natural, no matter where it falls on the gender spectrum.

CHARITIES

There are many groups of people around the world who try to improve social rights for transgender and non-binary people and help to prevent them from being discriminated against. One group in the UK that is well known for doing this is Press For Change. The people in this group try to make sure that all transgender people in the UK are respected and treated equally by their community.

These people gathered in North Carolina, US, in order to protest for the rights of transgender people.

Press For Change were one of the main **charities** to promote human rights for transgender people in the UK in the 1990s. Human rights are actions that all people should be allowed to perform simply because they are human. This means that everyone has human rights, no matter who they are and what their gender identity is. Over the last 30 years, many organisations and charities, including Press For Change, have tried to protect the human rights of transgender people. One of the most common ways that charities do this is by gathering at protests. This helps to raise awareness about transgender issues and shows people that the human rights of transgender people need to be protected.

Other charities and organisations around the world try to help by changing the way that societies view transgender and non-binary people. Unfortunately, there are some people who find it difficult to understand what it means to be transgender and non-binary. This can lead to discrimination towards those who identify as transgender and non-binary. Many organisations around the globe are trying to prevent this kind of discrimination from happening by teaching people about what it means to be transgender and non-binary. While there are still times when people are treated differently because of their gender identity, the world is becoming a more diverse, accepting and tolerant place all the time. It is extremely important to be accepting of others, regardless of their gender identity. No one should be afraid to be open with their gender identity

ACTIVITY

Can you think of all the things
that have shaped your identity?

GLOSSARY

activists   people who try to make social change by doing things such as holding protests

articles   pieces of writing that are included alongside others in a newspaper or a magazine

biological   relating to the body and how it works

charities   organisations that try to help people and don't make any profit

civilisations   the societies, cultures and ways of life of certain areas

contrast   to show how one thing is different from another thing

customs   traditional and widely accepted ways of behaving or doing things that are specific to a particular society, place, or time

discriminated   treated differently due to race, gender, religion, sex or age

equal   to be the same as

fundamental   something that is core or of central importance

genetics   to do with genes, which are small parts inside cells which have information on how to make specific parts of the body, such as hair or eye colour, and are passed from parent to offspring

morality   a person's sense of what is right and what is wrong

physical attributes   the features of your body, such as your height and the colour of your hair

protests   actions that express a disapproval of something, usually involving multiple people

respect   the consideration of the feelings, wishes and rights of other people

social construct   an idea that has been created and accepted by a society

spectrum   a scale with extremes at each end

stereotypes   assumptions that are made about a person because of their gender, sex, religion or nationality

tradition   a belief or way of doing something that has been passed down from one generation to the next

traits   a quality or characteristic of a person

unique   being the only one of its kind

INDEX